SEE US

COLORED, NEGRO, BLACK, AFRICAN AMERICAN, PERSON OF COLOR

Poems of Introspection and Observation

Ruby J. Jones, Ph.D.

Copyright © 2025 Ruby J Jones Ph.D.

All rights reserved. No part of this publication may be reproduced, distributed, or transmitted in any form or by any means, including photocopying, recording, or other electronic or mechanical methods, without the prior written permission of the publisher, except in the case of brief quotations embodied in critical reviews and certain other noncommercial uses permitted by copyright law.

ISBN: 978-1-960853-72-1

Cover Credit: Photo By Tim Mossholder Photos, Download The BEST Free Photo By Tim Mossholder Stock Photos & HD Images

Liberation's Publishing House – Columbus, MS

Dedication

First of all, for my sister, Mary Alvania, who has supported and encouraged me in all things. For my mother who taught me about God and education. For friends who have encouraged me over the years; you know who you are. Thank you, one and all!

Table of Contents

Part I Dreams and Disillusions 11
    Awakening 12
    Golden Promises 13
    Promises 14
    Crimes of the Heart 16
    Breezes 18
    Morning 19
    Hymn to Bacchus 20
    Mirrors 21
    Gifts 22
    Survival 23
    Lies 24
    Lessons Learned 25
    Night-time You 26
    Searching for You 27
    Till You 28
    Understanding 29
    Longing 30
    Inklings 31
    Comfort 32
    Priming the Pump 33
    Analysis of the Heart 34

Blues Redux 37

Love's Lament 38

Past into Future 40

Awakening 41

Shopping 42

Life Changes 43

Tears 44

Recidivism 45

Needs 46

Part II Struggling to Understand 47

   Same 48

   Amnesiacs in Waiting 49

   Poetry of the Soul 50

   Homeless 51

   Newton's First Law 52

   Basic Training Redux 53

   Green Machine, AKA Uncle Sam's Foundry 54

   Trash 55

   Game of Life 56

   Carriers 57

   Back the Blue 58

   Bloodline in Death 59

   Castalia- 1950s 60

   Mazes 61

Southern Chick-in 62
Autopsy 63
Little Saint 64
Personal Eternity 65
Ashes 66
Revolution 67
Shadowland 68
Anemia 70
Phantasm 71
Milton's Siblings 72
Delta 73
Pavlovian Response 74
Family Reunion 75
Mother Love 76
Manifest Destiny 77
Dialogue 78
Slaughterhouse 79
Orphan 80
Normality 82
A Black Knight 83
Tiger 84
A New Name for an Old Shame 85
Washed Clean 86
PTSD of a Non-combatant 87

Mirror Images 88
Test Taking / Exam Time 89
Linguistically Diverse 90
The Disciplinarian 91
Night in Georgia 92
The Forgotten 93
Faustian Perfection 94
Home 95
Genesis 96
Black by Definition 97
Depths 98
Life I 99
Eyes 100
Life II 101
Transitions 102
Panache (Je suis!) 103
Misfits 104
Late or Soon (Questings) 105
Touching 106
QWERTY 107
The Key 108
Mine and Mind 110
Nature Lover 111
Tristesse 112

3/5	113
Now	114
Silks	116
The Children	117
Times	118
Killer on the Prowl	119
Personal Analysis	120
Childhood Memories	121
The People	122
Monday, p.m.	123
Waiting	124
Mistake Eraser	125
Disjointed Thoughts	126
Words	127
Ignorance	128
Blues and My Father	129
Deep	130
Badge of Honor	131
Equality	132
Rewrite	133
Mortality	134
Nigra*	135
Introspection	137
Old Man	138

Hetero	139
Racism ... or what?	140
Sister	141
Religiosity	142
The Color of Power	143
Logic	144
Dieters Anonymous	145
The Thang!	146
Ode to a Pimple	147
Reflections of Self	148
Everybody Knows	149
Silence	150
Dandelion Wine (A Prequel)	151
Home	152
Stalker	153
Silence Redux	154
They	155
One Drop	156
Inheritance	157
Tennessee Women	158
Evolution – Devolution	159
About The Author	162

Part I Dreams and Disillusions

Awakening

This day, plain and ordinary to the rest of the world,

Brought sunshine and rain

And the other half of me into being.

For years without count, I searched.

Now I celebrate the day,

    the hour

        of your birth.

GOLDEN PROMISES

When last I lay with you,
The words were sweet
And promises golden.

Since last I lay with you,
The words are few
And the world is colder.

Since last I lay with you,
The time is long
And I am older.

                                        28 August 1976

Promises

I asked nothing of you,
But you promised the world,
At least as much of it as I wanted.
Now I sit alone in your dream world
Recalling the promises—empty again as always.

The new world is the same old world—
Cold and alone.
I asked nothing of you,
But you brought me alive—
Taught me to live and love and miss you,
Taught me to feel pain again,
To suffer the despair again.

I asked nothing of you.
Why did you come into my world
Bringing fear and pain again?
I had built beautiful walls—
Tall, strong, as old as time.
You—big, strong man—
Tore down in a day

What I took years to build.

Now I'm alone in this storm

Shedding tears I thought were forgotten,

Feeling pains I thought were dead.

I asked nothing of you;

You gave heaven and hell.

I asked nothing...

    You gave...

        I asked...

            You...

18 August 1976

Crimes of the Heart

I've waited and watched
Days and nights for the sight of you,
Even told myself I was dreaming
Though the sun was high.
I've played my childish games
For days without end,
Saying, "He will, he will not, he..."
Now comes reality—or another
Nightmare of disillusion.

The tears I will not shed
Are back again,
Making me ache, laugh too loud,
And die inside.
The years are rolling back—back
To other days, others times
When I felt the weight of
Crimes I never knew.

Time, never a gentle creature,
Is most ungentle with me,

Making me pay again and again

The price I cannot bear,

The price I should not bear.

The crime is birth;

The punishment, life;

The pardon, death.

27 August 1976

Breezes

The breeze kisses me tonight

Trying to fill the emptiness within me.

The hollow feeling is here,

That part of me is gone,

That maybe I'll find it —and you

Again tomorrow.

Still the breeze is sighing

Knowing she can't take your place.

The night is lonely still.

So, I'll take the breeze for comfort,

Let it fill my arms and dry my tears

Until you return.

27 August 1976

Morning

I'll never be so young again
As when I smiled and swallowed
All your lies.

The taste was sweet,
The time was smooth,
You were right

And I was wrong,
I was right
Lost inside your world.

But times changed and took me
Away from morning.

January 1976

HYMN TO BACCHUS

You drink to forget the pain
Which is all that is left for you.

Sweet oblivion:
Bacchus is my protector,
The guardian of peace of mind.

28 August 1976

Mirrors

I look in the mirror

And see you beside me.

I open my mouth

And hear you speaking love.

I touch my hair

And feel you caressing me.

My life had become so much

A part of you in so few days

That now it is barren—

Not even a reflection is left.

                                          29 August 1976

GIFTS

Clouds are a gift of yours,
Thunderstorms and gentle summer rain,
Sunshine promises and a legacy of pain—
Surprise gifts to last a lifetime.

Memories of happy times and waiting times
Balance each other
Within the passages of my mind:
Twisting memories, resurrected from
Crypts of marble, lie cold in the past.

                              30 August 1976

survival

I drank deep of you,

But I'll survive.

I listened to your promises,

But I'll survive.

I wait to hear from you,

But I'll survive.

I cry a little each night,

But I'll survive.

I die a little inside,

But I'll survive.

I gave my soul to you,

But I'll survive.

Strength is the essence of me,

So, I survive.

Willow mind, cypress body,

I always survive.

2 September 1976

Lies

You lied about the time of life and love
And about you and me.
Now I'm lying to myself
Taking your place in the scheme of things.

I cannot believe you bought with tawdry words
What I would so freely have given.
Were I to let myself believe it,
The pain would start again—going to infinity.

So, instead, I lie:
Burning bright yellow, bright red,
Flaming lies which consume
The pain and the agony.

14 September 1976

Lessons Learned

I'm still learning
The old wives' tales are lies:
Day cannot shatter pretense.
Sun and chatter hide all the
Lies I live.

But each day ends
And night drifts in with truth,
Quiet, pain and time:
Time to think, time to dream,
Time to suffer
The lies you lived.

Gentle, game-playing days;
Cold, truth-facing nights:
Nights—a learning time.

22 September 1976

NIGHT-TIME YOU

I've tried so many ways
To say you lied,
That I don't care.
But each night I come full circle:
The sunshine hatred
Becomes moonlight love.
The faith I bury each day
Rises with the moon
Whispering, "Fool, foolish child."

Love is stronger than my doubt,
More alive than my fear.
Memories come with the night—
Sweet gentle memories of time beyond call
When your face promised happiness beyond time.

So, now I wait for night,
    ...for you.

27 September 1976

Searching For You

Do you look for me in each new crowd

Because you miss the sight of me?

Can you hear me laughing through a door

Because the sound of me is still near to you?

Can you see me smile at your sleeping body

Because it is so dear to me?

Can you feel me beside you at night

Loving you, maybe teasing a bit?

If so, it's only fair,

Because I feel you.

10 October 1976

TILL YOU

Ice maiden running free,

Pain could never touch me,

Till you.

Controlled mind, living alone,

I called my soul my own

Till you.

From the world standing apart

No one could touch my heart

Till you.

                                                        8 November 1976

Understanding

Do you understand, my love,
The need I have for you?
This feeling, so new, so strange,
Has changed my life for good,
Or ill, but for always.
My love is only my life:
It shows in all I am or do.
I cannot show my love except
As I am—the product of my days.
I love you honestly,
As I am honest with myself.
I love you freely,
As I am free with myself.
The sum of my love for you
Can be no less than my love for self.

Can you understand, my love,
The need I have for you?

25 November 1976

LONGING

The touch of you, the taste of you

is like the sun I've seldom seen.

Now I miss the sunlight, the air,

the essence of you.

                              5 December 1976

INKLINGS

The silence is too loud—

or not loud enough—

to quiet the fear within me:

that you loved me less

or not at all.

The words of love are cheap to sell,

the deeds of love are hard to find.

                                              3 March 1977

comfort

My one-body bed is colder
than ever before.

Blankets and comforters
do not comfort the long hours

without you beside me.

                                                31 August 1977

Priming the Pump

I give and give

Until I'm almost dry.

Then, you prime me again,

so I can give some more.

All my stores are pumped

into your life,

leaving mine barren—

                almost.

                              5 September 1977

Analysis of the Heart

My hair,
ruffled and spiked from too much foundling,
is reflected in your slumberous and sensuous eyes,
until they close—
and I am alone with my thoughts, and yours.

Our meeting was stilted,
our parting will be painful—and what comes between?
'Tis too much of long sorrows and niggling doubts
to be wiped out by the transient joys.
Questions of my love and your love
that we fear to ask
still haunt this night of sexual pleasure.

The times I cried when you weren't around,
the times I cried when you held me close,
and laughed away the tears I could not hide;
oh, I wondered about your love for me,
but in my heart, I knew that the love was there.
If I could hold on to my love and to you long enough,

I could wipe out fear and questions,
and leave you free to love me—for me.

My eyes go slowly
from my mind to your sleeping eyes,
and the thoughts chase this night
to replace it with another night of hidden tears,
and accusations voiced out of fear
of losing me and me losing you.

And so, we fight like the cornered animals we are,
cowed by the essence of the power
we sense in each other,
power we freely gave that day we first embraced.

There was no doubt then,
only the awareness of what and who we were,
and wonder at the beauty and finality of our love—
Our love, the only one in the world,
so right, so ordained, so timeless.
But the time is now,
and I am now, here beside you in the dark,
watching the arms that held me tight,

hold tighter to old fears and doubts,

wrapping them around you

to keep away the warmth of my love and faith.

3 April 1977

BLUES REDUX

Somebody, help me live through this agony:

Blues with my father, lies with my lover.

                                                            20 December 1977

Love's Lament

You gotta love me
'cause I'm lovable.
I'm sweet and kind
and I know my own mind.
I'm the best you'll find
anywhere.
At least,
that's what people say.

So, you gotta love me,
'cause I'm careful
to give you everything you want,
everything you need—
even when you don't know
what, but
I care:
that's what people say.

Please, you gotta love me
'cause I'm part of you,
and you're all of me

and I build my life around you,

bind you with my arms,

my old charms,

my rare soul;

that's what people say.

Come on, you gotta love me!
WHY DON'T YOU?!

9 November 1977

Past Into Future

Loving and losing have become such a part of my life
That all I feel now is regret that the pattern
Continues until infinity.

The past forever reaches to threaten and engulf
The future that was so bright.

I play the fool so well, I can hardly believe
That it is all a lie I lived to change my life
Into yours, and into ghosts of your past.

awakening

came the dark,

the awakening from dreams;

and I saw you for the first time

as you are and not as I wanted you.

                                          23 December 1977

SHOPPING

Window shopping again

'cause the prices are high,

and the money is low,

and I just ain't found the change

to buy a man again.

19 April 1978

LIFE CHANGES

changes in my life flow

along tandem currents

carrying parts of me

and parts of you:

    I wonder what became of us.

20 May 1978

Tears

That I wept for me in silent ecstasy

made the tears no less painful.

And they flow,

cutting a path new and wide

to be later filled with

any dream I can find.

But, I never learn that

the tears are cheap

and the wounds too deep:

they swallow your dreams.

30 May 1978

RECIDIVISM

I knew the night would be cold;
So, I sheltered in your mind,
Wrapped your dreams around me
And waited for morning.

I knew the day would be lonely;
So, I crept into your life,
Let your heat surround me
And waited for night again--
        Alone.

I knew my life would be empty;
So, I crept into his mind,
Sheltered in his life,
And let my conscience cleanse me again—
        Ready for the next time.

Needs

Now and anytime, I need you--
To shut out the world and words,
The people who hold pain so cheap,
Doubt so trivial,
That they give it freely to one and all.

Part II Struggling to Understand

Same

We ain't the same;
It's a brand-new game.
Yesterday's rules
Are so "Old School."

Look at all these faces
From all kinds of places.
Let's get together and celebrate.
Learning from one another is simply great.

Close your eyes and look within;
Only you know where you have been:
How you walk, how you talk,
How you learn, what makes you burn.

Now open wide and look outside:
Your *self* is not the only source of pride.
The intelligences of people are oh so wide.
So, let your light shine; there's no need to hide.

Amnesiacs in Waiting

Susie Q, she drink she do:
an ocean of painkiller,
a pint of amnesia.

Her world lost its shape
last year or last month—or yesterday.
She breaks starch today in the bottom of a can.

Mary mine, she shine, she shine
Her dross soul echoes
In sympathy with men's suffering.

Your quest and her salvation become one,
In the reflection from her brassoed* mind.

Soul-gripping, ego-tripping on your minds,
She flits and flutters from man to man--
Using their quest for her salvation.

---

*Army slang, meaning bright and polished, i.e., cleaned and polished with Brasso©, a metal polishing product.

POETRY OF THE SOUL

A hand
      within the deepest stillness of me
          takes my soul

And leaves behind a tear.

Poetry of the soul
Does not exist in mediocrity:

One laughs hysterically
Or weeps with utter desolation.

HOMELESS

Tatters, flapping in the chill breeze,
Bits of cloth which barely cover a tattered life,
Shreds of dreams which went awry,
Have faded into weak shadows of themselves.
Once strong and vibrant, they clutter my path.
These tatters block the way forward.

Newton's First Law

Sweet morphic haze of life,
Fragile, lazy days of life
Drift in a cesspool of maladies,
Sifted from corridors of the mind.

Malcontent, but well-contented
To ooze a vita-plegia
Contaminating all who touch,
Emanating from a putrid source
Deep within the well of ego—
Ego-centered, egomania, ego-malady.
Childlike exclusion of all but self,
Centers the world around
The axis of her own self-indulgence.

She died eons ago,
The body still too lazy to change:
Newton's First Law of Motion.

Basic Training Redux

The time has been too short,
The memories, too rare,
To allow for trivial words.
The frustrations and shared anxieties
Are over—to start again
At another place in time.

In the end it was good:
The dawn-bound shivers and yawns
Are given up for nights under a different sky.
The faces change from day to day,
Growing more shadowy with each change,
Repeating the pattern to infinity.

Green Machine, AKA Uncle Sam's Foundry

And the green machine rolls on
Taking, making some, killing others.
And the weak will never survive
Unless in a myopic fantasyland.

And the weak ones roll on,
On into the machine they cannot fight.
Free room, free board, free minds:
Free of hate, free of pride, free of thought—
The ultimate freedom of will.

And the strong ones roll on,
Shaping the machine they will not fight.
Free as a Quixote of the soul,
A Prometheus of the mind,
They are bound by the freedom they seek
And the pride they hold.

Trash

Tarnished birds,
Molting through the years,
Competing with street chicks
In the dark,
In the park.

Game of Life

Play the game and live the lie.
Play their rules or you will die.
Play it straight and still you're wrong:
The weakest link is ever so strong.

Tell the truth and buy their scorn,
Tell a lie and they're glad you were born.
Play their game and what've you got?
You win a few and lose a lot.

You lose your pride, your reason for living;
You learn to take and forget the giving.
You die each day just to stay alive;
The strongest ones can barely survive.

So, take a chance and keep on trying:
The price you pay is a one-time dying.

Carriers (Reflections on a Border Tour)

Walls and fences
For your life and mine:
Only the water is free
To carry the thoughts of the past.

And the water shall carry it all:
The blood of the young
Mixes inexorably with debris from other dreams.
Karl's hand floats along with the current—
No longer shaping a vase or a train—
The tendons withered by fear and doubt.

But the water still carries it all:
The severed limbs and fish-dead eyes
Make a dirgeful pilgrimage
Away from life into a fantasy world
Of horrors less frightening than reality.

Forever the water carries it all
Beyond your walls and into my mind
Where I must carry it to eternity.

Back the Blue

"Back the Blue!"
No matter what they do.
"Love thy neighbor!"
As long as he looks like you.

Fun house mirrors distort reality's frame
Until only the shadows of shame remain.
Warped visions of another's reality
Where only self holds sway over justice.

Justice for self alone:
All others are on their own
In this carnival of horrors,
Free to suffer, die or limp along
The path of a life shaped and born out of others'
Hatred and greed.

What planted the seed?
Is it the crop of merely a weed
That chokes out the promise
Encoded in blood and skin
Encoding a humanity most central to our being?

BLOODLINE IN DEATH

Family in name unites over death.
We come together to echo the blood which ties,
But does not unite.
We each tread our separate paths until death,
The uniter of all, calls us once again
To pay homage to a shared history.

The guilty laughter and shamed smiles battle
With the sense of loss, or non-loss,
Of a blood-bound stranger.

Theatrics interrupt the flow,
The smooth and quiet transition
From one plane to the next.
They shift the focus from the central player
In our mortality play
To another, lesser sharer of the blood.
The bloodline sharer takes center stage in diminished form.

Castalia- 1950s

Rows of newly-built apartments stretch beyond the horizon
Of a small child's vision and imagination.
They are such a contrast to the one back room
Shared in someone else's house.

Not so far away, just across the tracks,
Out of sight, but not out of sound, begins a new life.
Newly paved streets cannot erase the same old habits
Brought along with the new furniture.

I cross the tracks, pass by the former home,
En route to the new school,
To future's narrow gateway.

                                          11 November 2023

Mazes

I run from myself in a crooked maze of old ideas,
Afraid to let me find myself,
Afraid that my sensitive fingers would find my soul
And probe the excrement of my life.

Still, I run and run like a mouse in a maze:
Amazed that I don't learn the turns and twists,
Amazed that around one corner I see I,
Around another, I run into me,
Amazed that I run from the reflection of myself
Into another maze of half-dreams and horrors.

                                        January 1975

SOUTHERN CHICK-IN

Are you half so dumb as now you seem?
Or are you playing a deep game
Within your little mind?

You step on my ego to hold yours high.
It is enough that I am strong,
Can smile at your puerile antics:
The pseudo-smiles, the friendly hands
That shirk too close a contact
With inferior beings,
Except to feed the flames
Of all your yesterdays' glory.

February 1976

AUTOPSY

So, I'm dead.

Now my soul itself is exposed to your microscopic stare.
Dissect it all and record the results in sterile lab books.
Place the hate on a slide:
It can be no more ugly than when I breathed.
Now, you've located the nucleus.
Try to separate my fear from the cause of my death.

Cut and slice and dye and decant
Until you find the surprising essence of me.
Add a milliliter of acid and find my best element.
Do you find any love, maybe a bit of compassion,
Or is the best only a hodgepodge of apathy
Which remains intact despite all the tests?

Perhaps you find a sliver of prejudice.
Once I shielded all its corrosive power;
But now I'm dead and you control the locks.
Can you find the key and reseal my soul
Before I destroy the world?

Poor, lonely pathologist, is it worth all your wasted effort?

January 1975

Little Saint

And, if you're bad...

Your suffering will wash away all your sins.
Your lies will set you free.

Little Saint, you pile your guilt upon me
Brick by dirty brick until
The weight crushes me.

And gives you wings to shimmer
And shine blinding lights,
Crippling lights leaving only
Memories of perfection.

January 1976

Personal Eternity

The Sun rose, and died screaming,
Begging to complete another day
Without the insufferable agony
Of oblivion:

To forever shine,
To know eternity ...
    For a little while.

But the moon must also rise
To taste gently of its eternity.

October 1970

ASHES

The fires of passion are banked:
Out of the ashes rises a new Black man,
Coming like a phoenix, but vulture-visaged,
To reap the spoils of an era.

Nat, your brother did not die in the revolution:
He dies of the plague,
Destroyed by the germs of hate and fear.
"The" revolution is over, the soldier's back home,
On the streets, but still fighting.
The enemy's name is now "brother" –
Black on Black against Black.

Shed tears of sorrow, tears of rage,
For all the beautiful Black men.
To what nether regions have they flown,
All your high ideals, your revolutionary zeal?

						December 1974

Revolution

Revolution has a color.
It's neither black,
Nor brown,
Nor red,
Nor yellow,
Not even the color of blood.

The color of revolt is green
For growth
And birth
And spring into eternity—
The shadowed green of despair.

January 1976

SHADOWLAND

The shadows of emotion
Are all I know,
Deep, unseen, growing darker
As the years pass me by.

Today I feel the years
And watch them
Leave the tracery of time
Upon my face.

The shadows painted beneath my eyes
Show a landscape of increasing dreariness,
Rain-covered emotions,
Growing stronger with time,
Reflected in street puddles,
Intensified by repetition:

Carnival mirrors distort reality
And cast monsters in my wake.

February 1976

Vocamus*

We call
For the death of strangers
And the tears of lovers.

We call
You the enemy, the spoiler,
The killer of all our dreams.

We call
Ourselves
"Vox populi."

And we feel no pain,
For the world is ours.
We are the world,
And you are not.

27 February 79

Latin, "we call"

Anemia

Such an anemic blue for the top of the world,
Such a pale anemic gray for the top of my life.

The sky is weighing me down,
The people pressing me down,
Fading me to shades
Of myself reflected
In myriad fragments
Against the pale sky,
Against their lives, paler still.

December 1975

PHANTASM

Except the world at a slower pace
Would rule my life,
Lay down new laws
To seal my dreams,
I would
Become a giant,
New-grown, full-blown thing
Of nature
Controlling the day.

I would
Shape your life,
Sell your dreams
To fill a pipe of ashes:
Ashes of repentance,
Ashes of death—
Caustic ash of life.

February 1976

MILTON'S SIBLINGS

Milton's siblings exist in a world apart,
A world where death or life has no meaning.
There is no change, only the continuance of
things past.
All the lost innocents play a serious game
Of survival of the weakest.

They sing and dance a dervish madness,
Tangling in age-old schizoid traps,
While the children who might have been,
The young innocents never conceived,
Smile as they dream of hell—

They dream and see this planet Earth.

September 1974

Delta

I have been as young and as old
As time could warrant.
Faced with the wisdom of age,
I have taken the way of an infant.
My tears fell when time told me to fight.
I tried to resist and still flow with the tide.

And yet, life has forced me to change.
Even as the seasons revolve,
Ever returning to the spring of rebirth,
So changes my psyche:
One day, young and happy as verdant spring,
Another, old and frightened as autumn's gray--
Mutable days of hopes and frustrations,
Loves and hates, defeats and victories,

Days that speak of changes yet to come.

Pavlovian Response

Where is he,
This knight of the darkness,
My young mind's savior?
Has he wandered into someone else's life,
Given her the gifts I craved?

Maybe he, too, got lost in the turmoil of life,
Lost his way among the goals and achievements.
Does he even recognize my absence?
Can he imagine what I might have given,
Might have done for him?
For us?

Maybe the craving is just a Pavlovian reflex,
The should-haves, could-haves of society.
Maybe I should ask:
Where is me?

                                13 January 2024

Family Reunion

There are sisters, brothers, mothers, fathers,
Cousins beyond number.
All these critters from ancient bloodlines
Come together at this time, in this space
To complete the ritual dance of blood.
Can we be so alike and so different
In so many different ways that
Ancestors would cast us aside,
Disown us all as unworthy?
There's the doctor, the lawyer,
The drunk, the drug addict—
All share blood and memories.
The taint and the glory are equally shared,
Neither giving more than the other,
Neither being recognized as more worthy,
But bearing testament to the persistence of blood.

The root and seed are forever shared
Throughout the scattered family tree.

MOTHER LOVE

She might have held my hand:
She must have at some point.
I don't remember.
The hugs and kisses which seem so normal
Are absent from my memory.

The cozy talks, the counselling wisdom
Shared with a child,
Never materialized.
Symbols of emotions,
Pride of creation for outward show,
Are all that remain.

Pictures on the wall,
Proofs of what should have been,
Are all that remain.

Manifest Destiny

I have seen the beginning of all things.
I am eternal black
Strength grasping the axis of the world,
Making you revolve about my dust,
Swirling all before the winds of me.

I take you
North to death,
South to sorrow,
West to change,
East to hope.

I am all things:
Clouds are more substantial than I.
Mountains crumble before I shift.
I am sweeter, gentler than rain,
Colder than death:

I am you in colors of us.

DIALOGUE

God is Love. ...
        Or, so you say!

You gotta live this way:
      so came the Law from up above.

You just ain't right, you all gotta die:
Words writ in the Bible tell you why.

Who's judging?! Not me!
I just know what's right.
I've been to the river; I've seen the light!

I've been washed clean of all hate.
I'm blessed as can be.
Those rules you talk about,
Well, they just don't apply to me,

'Cause I've been blessed,
Washed clean of pride,
My blessed purity I cannot hide.

'Cause I've been blessed, don't you know?
"For the Bible tells me so."

SLAUGHTERHOUSE

The herd is gathering in the gloom,
Lining up for the feeding trough,
Pushing and clawing its way into
Oblivion.

A little more slop each day
Will keep the herd in line.
(The dieters will soon be gone.)

> Feed them fast,
> Feed them slow!
> Feed them poison –
> They won't know.

The herder is tipsy, but they don't know:
They think it's something in the blood.

And the blood must flow.

Orphan

Orphan child got up this morning
Looking for something:

Found a man,
Loved for a while,
Lied for a while,
And moved on.

Orphan child went to bed tonight
Still looking.

caverns

The days are creeping past
With the weight of years
And the pace of tears
Slowly welling from bloodshot caverns
Holding the shadows of yesterday's mistakes.

Caverns are part of my days:
Caverns to shape my life,
Caverns to hide my fears
From prying eyes and prying fingers
And prying minds.

Normality

Normality:
The questions without answers,
Or is it answers without questions?

It is the story of my life:
To care too much, or too little,
Is, equally, a sin.

A Black Knight

He only likes white-meat chicken,
This Black knight of the new world.
"Dark meat has no class,
Disturbs my digestion."
Nothing dark but his suits,
His cars,
His heart…

And skin;
But mirrors lie,
Or so he thinks.

Tiger

Lonely Yamashita sits in the dock
And thinks of all the years before
When he lived and loved and laughed,
The years before the world went berserk,
The years when pride and truth and honesty
Meant more than color of skin or slant of eye.

Poor Tiger, being ridden by the good
And the righteous and the holy
Guardians of truth and justice;
Riders who found their way to get off his back
And destroy the Tiger in one swoop—
Eagles, tracking and bagging the cat.

A New Name For An Old Shame

It would have been called a shanty near the land
Where my grandfather toiled on the soil.
This house has earned a new name
In this urban sharecropped land.
No ownership of anything,
And others wonder about the
Lack of care, lack of pride.
Shotgun houses of urban blight;
They couldn't even get that right.
Sharecropping leaves no room for pride.

                                                10 August 2024

Washed Clean

White Rose laundry promised clean and fresh.
It delivered washed and starched and ironed
Items to all the right people.

The wrong people left limp and drained
After a too-long day.

PTSD of a Non-Combatant
(The trauma of living in your world)

When the sun sets in this Sundown Town,
"Don't let your black ass be found!"
So, we shuffle, pound the ground,
Eyes lowered, but always looking around.

The danger lurks behind blue eyes
And friendly smiles on a pale face.
The smiles only shift if I fail to know my place.

20 July 2024

Mirror Images

What on earth will you finally do
When you realize that we are people just like you?
We lie, cheat and steal, have numerous flaws
But, if you look in the mirror or at your own,
You will see that they are also breaking laws.

Saints and sinners have no particular hue.
One quickly morphs into the other.
It all depends on your point of view.

27 June 2024

Test Taking / Exam Time

He stares into the nothingness of the blank page
And sees a reflection of more than pain.
It's the expectation of pain unanswered, of desires unvoiced.
The nothingness stares back and torments the soul,
Twists the reflection of self into monsters plumbed
From the depths of too-short a childhood's memory.

Linguistically Diverse

"Linguistically diverse" removes the soul of the subject,
Places them on a separate place far distant from your world
Of Strunk & White and Socrates.
Confucious would be confused by the myriad
Shapes of personalities swirling within the miasma of reality.
Each leaf on the branches of humanity's one tree
Buds and develops, takes shape guided by
Past, present and future hopes.
The soil, so common, shared by all, is roiled by feet
Trying to stamp the other out of existence.

5 May 2023

The Disciplinarian

Silence—a powerful weapon—walks in on confident legs,
Looks around with a quelling glare.
The murmurs still to underground rumbles of
Seismic shifts in consciousness.

The shallows reflect palpable currents of awareness inchoate,
The realization of humanity budding within a carapace
Of youth, as yet unbound by society's strict rules
Which bury the child and leave behind only silence.

7 May 2023

NIGHT IN GEORGIA

Gentle nights of quiet moods
Creep over Georgia.
They camouflage the obscenities of day.
Night, the pacifier, the comforter
Is the mother of Morpheus.

The Forgotten

They say
    That unimportant is easiest forgot.

People always forget that
    I laugh...

        I cry.

Faustian Perfection

One note of a bomb:
One, three buttons for destruction.

    Easy
        E-e-e-e-e-asy.

All is lost for one moment of perfection:
    Faust and his trumpet.

HOME

You can never go home again:
you left too long ago,
going in search of a different world,
    new dreams and ...
        something new,
anything for a change.

You arrived and found that:
    the world was still the same,
        the dreams as old as eternity.
    Everything was the same ...
        and changeless.

You can't go home again,
    and there's no place else to go.

Genesis

In the end it was as it should have been in the beginning.
Neither spoke of the things which had passed between them:
> No words of blame,
>> No thoughts of shame.

They had each been too many different people
For too many different reasons.

Recriminations would have answered none of the
Questions which haunted their silences:
Silences neither of comfort nor of peace.
Theirs was the silence of the damned...

> or of a new genesis.

Black By Definition

Black is the

    Night,

        Coal,

            Earth,

                Onyx,

                    Oil,

                        Ebony,

                            Sorrow,

                                Death...

ME!

DEPTHS

Fathom the depths of me,
My beauty and sorrow:
Beauty of the morning.
Sorrow in the night.

Exuberant smiles
Running toward another
To share the joy,

Gently flowing tears
Reaching for another
To ease the pain.

Life I

Dreams: weak creations of man,
A suckling infant
Fed on pablum and honey,
Nurtured and protected from life.

Desires: children born of necessity,
Cherished for a lifetime,
Never allowed to mature,
Never encouraged to live.

Reality: existing, complete within itself,
Neither asking nor expecting anything,
Needing only acceptance –not even that,
The thesis and culmination of dreams and desires.

eyes

Laughing eyes, crying eyes:
    Gentle heart.

Quiet eyes, hidden eyes:
    Strong heart.

Portals or walls,
Deep or shallow
Eyes of the soul,
Brown or black eyes,
Shouting for retribution,
Asking for change –
        My eyes.

Feel them laugh quietly in your heart,
Hear them cry in the hidden recesses of your mind.

My eyes, your eyes:
Living for the universe,
Existing with a star.

LIFE II

People running from life,
Borrowing umbrellas to protect themselves
From joy and sorrow.

Souls imprisoned in dreams and desires,
Refusing both sun and rain
Essential to growth.

Children forever...
    Playing games,
        Escaping reality,
           Afraid of the truth.

Transitions

I have touched the sky with a million different voices:
The voice of a child sleeping in the night,
The voice of a woman first tasting love,
The voice of a mother trying to calm another's fears.

I have walked the earth with a thousand different eyes:
The eyes of a child crying for lost innocence,
The eyes of a woman sighing for the love long dead,
The eyes of a mother seeing the loss of one never fully known.

All these have I been, all these have I seen:
They have been part of me since the beginning of time.
None of these have I known, none of these have I felt:
They shall be with me until the end of time.

I am, I will be
So much, so little,
So sad, so eternal.

Panache (Je Suis!)

I am that I am,
No more, no less;
Your dreams, your desires
Cannot change me.

I stand alone in
Awareness of myself;
Neither dreams nor desires
Control my destiny.

As I pass through the stages
Of yesterday and today,
I find the beginning of my life
Too near its inevitable end.

My mind records the days of vigilance,
Trying not to lose the essence of living.
Though I hear and see all,
I know only my limitations.

I am freedom
Such as no man has known.
I am love
Winging to heights of my own.

    I am serene.

MISFITS

They are not many who walk this path.
They sing and dance alone in the moonlight,
Delighting in a tree or the waning moon.
They have come through the doors of Time itself,
Anachronisms fighting for survival in the wrong world.
Born too late or too soon,
They struggle against destiny.

This, then, is their tragic flaw:
To be out of step with humanity,
To be crucified not for their own conceit
But for the machinations of capricious Time.

Late or Soon (Questings)

Ten years, more or less, from the hour of my birth—
Would it make such a change in total worth?
Would there live a stranger within this dusky skin,
Or would I be what I have always been?

Too soon, and would I care less
For the ideas I now profess?
Would I know more the spirit of man,
Or would I struggle under a darker band?

Would I have found a gentle place
To echo all of a people's grace,
Or would my life have been so grim
That I'd not see the love of Him?

Had I been born ten years late,
Would I again have learned to hate
All mankind, my own included?
Would no one be excluded?

Could I walk along and find
Some little good in all mankind,
Or would the world have changed to much
That not one person would I dare touch?

One decade, could it effect such drastic change
That I would not know the me that remains?

TOUCHING

We walk side by side, but never touching,
infinitely afraid to let the other know our pains
again.
For once we held hands and laughed about
yesterday,
Cried about tomorrow, to what end?
We held each other's lives in our eyes.
But, in the end you—or maybe I—
Abandoned what little trust we had
In exchange for other strings to bind us.

And so, we walk side by side, never touching.

QWERTY

Qwerty, qwerty, how I love thee,
Qwerty, qwerty, my old friend:
Fingers flying—such a joy:
No longer.

What's this in my hand?
So small and light! I don't understand.
Qwerty, qwerty—is this the end?
Qwerty is gone:
   Now I hit 'send'.

THE KEY

The key lies tarnished in the dust.
She lost it yesterday, or the day before,
Or maybe some other time that she can't recall.
She didn't even know it was gone.
There were too many other things
To occupy her mind and energies:
The price of gas for her next vacation,
The color of her dress for the club dance,
These and other essentials of her existence.
She covered her head in burlap from her own mill
And wondered why she couldn't see the sun,
Why the stars hid behind clouds at night.
One autumn, when winter threatened her life,
She began to check all her summers' work
And found she had mislaid one small key.
She searched and scrambled among
The money and the clubs and the card games
And the charities and the status symbols—
And came away clutching a handful of nothing.
Trying to recreate the scene of her loss,
She couldn't remember when she saw it last:
Whether she had it when she got her degree,

Or if she lost it in the new car,
Or maybe it fell into the Rhine or the Loire.
The white cat still stalks his prey,
While she stumbles in the autumn dusk
Looking for the key lying at her feet.

MINE AND MIND

He stands, tall and proud,
Daring the wind to cease his blowing.
He sits, angry and defiant,
Telling the sea to change her flow.
He plans to stop the world from destroying itself.
Quietly producing beauty,
He gives to the world a part of his soul.

He is all these things—or maybe none.
He has been there, beyond the sunrise,
Since the beginning of time,
Waiting for me.

Will he touch my awareness
That I may know him when he comes
Or will all my yesterdays' dreams
Cloud the view and leave me wondering?

Nature Lover

Let the trees caress me with long slender fingers.
The grass will cradle my weary head
While I make love to the sky.

The sun, behind a cloud, smiles at my ecstasy.
He shines on others, but to me
He gives a warm kiss of love.

His brother Sky penetrates my very soul,
Bringing to me new joys undefined.
My body answers the love and strength
That pours forth from him.
All my longings find an answer
In his searching sensuality.

But, so often have I dreamed of this joy,
That ecstasy is becoming insanity,
Or insanity becomes ecstasy,
Or ...

Tristesse

Loneliness and I walk hand in hand,
Surveying the landscape of the world.
We watch lovers strolling at twilight
Making plans for more tomorrows together.
An old woman nods as we pass,
Still lost in memories and dreams of yesterday.

But loneliness only speaks to me.
He asks about my fears and sadness.
And I whisper to him
    of home
        and love
            and quiet comfort …

And parts of dying dreams.

3/5

Three-fifths is such an awkward thing to be.
You can't stand right.
You can't sit right,
You can't even lie right—
Except to lie to the boss
About where the extra stuff went,
And what you did at home last night.

Tell him all the lies he loves to hear,
Until the weight of your lies
Traps him in the ignorance of his world.

NOW

Enjoy while you can, the pleasures of life.
For night calls us to tranquility too soon
And we lose all tragic depths of feeling.
Now is all we have,
This fleeting break in time,
To be all that we were or shall be,
To live all dreams, fulfill all promises.

Tomorrow, the wraith of time,
Steals all the fruits of reality
And leaves us floundering in the answers
To each other's paradise.

But, the tortured path for you veers right
Away from the rain forests through which I tread.
The doors of your path were opened
Or slammed in your face
By choices alien to me.
So, don't give me the guilt you cannot face,
The sins you cannot expiate.

My sins are heavy leviathan creatures,
Binding me to old guilts and spurious emotions.
Their weight keeps me earthbound.
I would share all your burdens,
But we must each bear our own choices,

Face the past and future equally,
Shunning no responsibility for today.
For now is all there is:
Yesterday is already a memory,
Tomorrow, but a promise.

SILKS

The gaudy, sometimes tawdry threads
Are tangled amid the pins and sins
Of my gaudy, sometimes tawdry life.

THE CHILDREN

The children laugh,
While the world is gay.

The children cry,
While the world is sad.

The children die,
When the world is blind.

TIMES

There are times when you feel like crying,
Though you know the tears are all gone.
They were wasted on trivials and incidentals:
Trembling is all that is left for you.

Killer on the Prowl

You can kill this body, but the spirit within is free,
Free of the fear which is killing you daily.

Fear brings a little death each time you see my face,
A face dark with pride and history.
It shows rivers of life, rivers of death,
Separated more by years than by miles.
Proud, muddy rivers, proud bloody rivers
That overflow their banks with the history of me,
While you are muddin' on the banks,
Afraid to enter the flow which can bury your fear
As you could not bury me.

Personal Analysis

The thousand and one yesterdays cannot be erased.
You are where you stand today with the accumulation of
All your sins and virtues.
They are part of all you are.
If they could be shed, there would still remain …
Not innocence, but a thin layer of skin
Revealing vulnerabilities and imperfections.

CHILDHOOD MEMORIES

Childhood's memories have shrunk in size
As I review with an adult's eyes:
The old streets are not half so long,
The old emotions, not half so strong.

THE PEOPLE

For the people
We take freedom
From the people,
And give death
To the people.

We, the people!

MONDAY, P.M.

The nothing, neverness of my past
Drenches the city,
And paints the sidewalks a somber gray.

Lost chances have flooded the gutters of my mind,
Flooded gutters of age and time:
Even the sky cries for thing I never did.

Waiting

Waiting time is hard time.
The limbo of mind time
Casts shadows
Growing with each minute
To wipe out hope
And plant fear with each breath.

Waiting time is crying time.
A little bit dying time
Grays the heart,
Seeping life's blood drop by drop,
Anemic tones of life,
Coloring the paler shades of existence.

Waiting time is waiting
    For me
        To wait
            Alone.

Mistake Eraser

Change the times of my life
To the times of your life.
Change the cares of my life
To the cares of your life.
Change the soul in my life
To the soul in your life.
Change me
To reflections of you,
To nothing.

Better to begin again at nothing.
Erase all tragic mistakes,
Implode me out of the cosmos
With no debris to mock my going.

Then smile
For all good changes.

DISJOINTED THOUGHTS

Of what use is a name?
It is all that stands between me and the void of nonexistence.
It changes nothing, the names you give to me.
The name I give myself is all.

Honeyed words, hackneyed words trip
through the corridors of my mind.

Something stirred deep within me;
I think I'll call it God.
Something touched me with fingers of ease;
I think I'll call it Death.

I was when you wallowed in antediluvian mud.
I shall be when your robots and clones are
But the dust which swirls about my feet.

Playing games is not for the children of this world:
The young are too innocent to learn the rules.

words

Words is the bridge from me to you:
Baby's first cry,
The dying's last sigh.

Nigger is a word.
Honky is a word.
LGBTQ+ is a word.

Words is us.

16 June 2019

Ignorance

Ignorance is a virtue: it's all the rage.
How did we all so easily
come to this page
of history's truth as lie,
victor as victim?

Now we all pay the price.

                                          21 November 04

Blues and My Father

The time was long
In coming and going,
When I sang the blues
So long ago.

Train whistles sang along with me
In the accompanying dark—
Shades of tears
That were only shed in later years.

Time was out of joint—
When the young were old,
And the old were young
And blues was the tune of life.

Smoldering coals, soot of childhood's dreams:
Dirty memories that birthed the blues.

Deep

My people:

pale, pale,

reflecting light;

dark, dark,

promising night

smiles and frowns,

tears and fears,

deep down

whirling 'round

within --

all the same,

all different,

all one.

Badge of Honor

the white badge of honor –

so bright, so right.

shields your sins

and guards your world

from such as I –

    shadow child,

shaped by you,

    aped by you.

EQUALITY

We, too, be angels
>   black and gleaming,
and demons unparalleled—
>   glowing in shades and tones of evil.

Rewrite

All the pains,
    all the gains –
        rewrite.

Forget the mean,
    make it clean –
        rewrite.

The blood is gone,
    but not the song –
        rewrite.

When dreams must die,
    the old will cry –
        rewrite.

The young ones rage
    when on the page
        of history
            is writ
                the lie.

Lest we forget –
    Re-right!

10 January 1998

Mortality

Mortality is in my mind—
Not yours, or theirs,
But mine.

When night sneaks in
And defenses are lowered,
When each body's creak or rumble is
Death's inevitable whisper,
Then come the silent words,
The hidden words—
In strength proportionate to our joys—

Not me, anyone but me!

Nigra*

I rocked many a cradle with these calloused hands.
I soothed your body and eased your mind
Before you knew you were alive.

I fed you on the history of you and me and mine.
Without words
I crooned away the death and breath of agony
With a low moaning sound.

I gave you milk of kindness and clabber of gall
To make you grow
Tall and brown and black and sad.

I gave you me in all the shadows of day,
Shielded you from their sun

---

* black (Latin, adj, fem, sing)

Until you were strong enough to live
Without my shade.

Yea, I rocked your cradle
Gave you my strength, my blood,
My voice, cracked with age,
My body, bent with age.

What did you give me?

Introspection

Halcyon days of quiet reflection,
A time of growth and introspection.

The eternities of my life meander ceaselessly:
They bring solitudes and multitudes,
Joys and sorrows.

My soul, as Lazarus, reawakens from sorrows,
Death-bearing sorrows torturing soul and body.
Yet, does my sorrow temper my psyche,
Making me strong, malleable.

Thus, can I appreciate joy when it comes,
Joy to lighten the load of remembered sorrows.
Joy brings the birth of new ideas—new dreams,
Borne from the ashes of sorrow.

OLD Man

Poor, foolish Lear,

He has dreamed such dreams as leave him weak,

Weak with the realization that what he sought

Was never intended to be,

That his dreams were the child

Of utopian imaginings.

Foolish man,

Dreaming of justice and love and piety,

Dreaming, only to wake to the aridity of his existence.

Lear drowns in the icy eyes of childhood.

He has grown old, but not wise,

Ancient, and still he dreams,

        dreams,

    dreams.

Hetero

we are normal,
      we are right,
we are hetero,
      we are white.

the past—
it never was,
it will not die;
the future—
      as we see it
      gives birth to the lie:

all are equal,
      we know—ours is the game.
if you chose to be different,
      yours is the shame.

Racism ... or What?

I can destroy—
    feel my strength!
I can kill—
    feel my rage!
I can wipe you all
    from history's page.
I am all-white,
    can go to any length,

to prove my might,
    my right,
        my white soul of purity
and rot...

'cause that's all I've got.

sister

this blood we share from ages past
has built a bond that's bound to last

life's puzzle:
the years of strife,
the days of toil,
are surely part of life

'til we all rest in the soil
of home,
and heart,
and family dear

whose blood will prove...
that we were here.

RELIGIOSITY

So what if they got no soul;
Religion's still the best control.

He'll save you,
　give you all you need
　　in heaven ... someday.

and my
God laughed about promises
　yet to be kept, ...

　　　and debts yet to be paid.

The Color of Power

Does anyone recognize the true color of power?
Do we assign an unchosen color for all times?
Will it become as iconic as the dirty blues,
As white as hot rage,
As yellow as cowardice,
Or as green as envy?

Black death comes to all:
Color of skin neither protects
Nor condemns to one immutable fate.

Color permeates our world and our minds.
The rainbow envelopes us in adamantine arms.
The inner eye discerns subtle changes,
Emanations from out of the depths,
Emanations which echo the substance of our perceptions.

The colors flow down from the past,
Through history's songs of rape and conquest,
Of defiance and submission.

The color of power changes with time, but never dies:
The putrid stench of decay remains and lingers
In the air above the corpse of all our hopes.

LOGIC

Your logic has a fatal flaw.
This is not what you thought you saw.
The actors all had another plan:
Unwavering support for just one man.

The lies pile up stone by stone.
Their weight is enough to shatter bone.
They bury your doubts under layers of words.
The devastation cuts deeper than swords.

Dieters Anonymous

Balloon-body crying empty
Suffer a cause
To seize a goal
Cry for chicken, golden fried;
Cry for lemon, meringue-pied.
Stomach growling, midriff bulging,
Suffer in silence, suffer a lie:
I'm not as good with five pounds over.
I'm not as fit to find a lover.
Growling, grumbling child of time,
Much more beautiful an aeon ago.
Agonies of poverty,
Trademark of need.
Add a layer of fat each day,
The more fat, the more the soul's decay,
Putrefied by society's scorn.
Fat—a bane, a balm, a sin of life:
Condemned by the pure and righteous
Daughters of slim.

The Thang!

The symbol ain't the thang,
but it's so damn close,
close enough to heaven,
or as close as I want,

as close as I'll get,
with you weighing me down,
bringing me down,
pulling me back down

to be me,
all over again
as I was then,
as I will ever be.

Can't you see?
it's really me.

I'm the thang.

ODE TO A PIMPLE

Center face, and proudly glisten,
Oh, how you shine,
And how I love you,
This third eye of mine.

You came one day
From out of the blue
And stayed for weeks—
Not very long, but who knew?

You will not go,
But linger on and on.
What will I do,
When you're finally gone?

Maybe in a hundred years or so,
You'll finally give up and die,
And I can put an end
To this ode to a pimply third eye.

02 June 2005

Reflections of Self

The strange reflection of self
I see in alien eyes
Overwhelms the person I thought I knew.
This stranger within my dusky skin
Shudders and shakes, but does not break
Beneath the judgement in those eyes.

The reflection is not more powerful
Than the essence of self.
As I walk the streets of the city
I find my twins flowing to meet me—.
In the middle of this carnival mirror world.

EVERYBODY KNOWS

Everybody knows that night humours can destroy a strong body against its will.
Everybody knows that invisible forces cannot possibly kill.
Everybody knows that They are the eternal enemy
Come to rampage, steal and kill you and me.
Everybody knows that this is the best that has ever been.
To say otherwise should be considered a mortal sin.

Everybody knows that your mind ain't right.
Otherwise, you'd agree with me and come to see the light.
Everybody knows that words don't matter:
The lies are a balm to make the ego feel better.
Everybody knows that 'woke' destroys traditions.

Everybody knows what nobody knows.

SILENCE

Silence wraps herself around me.
Silence shuts out horrors and hurrahs.
Silence traps me in a vault of introspection.
She shines a light on gifts and imperfections.

Silence is the mirror of my soul.

Dandelion Wine (A Prequel)

Poor, dainty-looking dandelion, coming up through cracks in the driveway.
Unwanted encroacher from alien realms,
This yellow invader pushes up through the smallest cracks,
Overcomes all obstacles.

There's such a small crack through which to move.
"You're so stupid. Can't you do anything right?"
The yellow petals struggle to burst through.
"I told you how to do it. And you still got it wrong!"
The hardy green leaves on the stem
Unfurl with a hungry yearning for light.
"Go back and do it again! Tell them exactly how I told you!"
Finally, the yellow petals are reaching for the yellow sun,
While her essence waits, ferments under the stress,
Waiting for the day when her life
Becomes fine like wine.

HOME

Home waits for me.
Home, where have you been all these years?
Someone promised that I would have you,
Love you, cherish you.
Did you sneak off with another and leave me
Alone in the house we shared?

Stalker

The tracks of this animal do not fade with time.
It stalks its prey, with purpose.
Neither rain nor tears can wash away
The depressions left in the soil of the soul.

The predator seems immortal and immoral.
He stalks his prey, leaves his footprints,
Marks his territory with scent and scat,
Befouling the existence of alien eyes.

The stalker does not waver, does not weaken.
His purpose is his strength.

SILENCE REDUX

Silence screams its presence, its quiet power
To steal comfort from the stillness of inner thoughts.
Silence magnifies the absence of other,
Illuminates the darkness of empty spaces.
Silence tiptoes and slinks into corners of the mind
Which others have abandoned.
The shadows cast by missing voices and bodies
Are loud enough to shatter the primordial unity of self,
The long-cherished ideas of who and what
We were before your intrusion into
This solitary monolith of existence.

Only silence remains to remind us of other realities and regrets,
Remorseless stones cast into the flowing current of a life.

THEY

They are swarming all around.
They will put me in the ground.
They populate my nightmares and dreams.
But, are they really what they seem?

They are us!

One Drop

'One drop' is such a piddling thing.
One drop of rain cannot transform a desert
Into lush forests of hope.
One drop of honey cannot soothe a throat
Or sweeten a life.

But when I look in the mirror,
Accusing reflections stare back—
Remnants of bygone ages, now splintered into shards of hate
Which reverberate into the present and
Filter through cracks in the psyche of a nation.

That one drop of blood straight out of Africa—
Strong enough to survive the Middle Passage—
Overwhelms all other blood,
Conquers all, vanquishes all,
Transforms human into animal, man into myth—
Unworthy, unloved, yet undaunted.

One drop flows down through generations,
Leaving a stain on the psyche of history's victims,
Leaving a twisted image in the psyche of history's victors:
Two worlds constructed from the detritus of one drop of blood.

Inheritance

We, inheritors of the past,
Gifts spewed out of history's maw,
Have no chance or choice
But to wade and waddle through
The strictures placed around us.

We, the demonized, otherized
Emblem of a past obscured by lies
And fantasies, pace forward with
Head held high into a future
Of unfathomable, vaunted changes.

We, the whipping boy, phantasm of all your fears,
Reflect onto your carnival mirror
All the secrets you dare not admit,
All the crimes you call goodwill,
Twisting everything into new monsters of hate.

Tennessee Women

We come here from different pasts, families, heritages all.
We grew up in cities, towns, on farms or on mountains tall.
Our differences shatter under the awesome weight
Of our lifelong battles against the politics of hate.

In the quiet stillness of night
They still try to hide us out of sight.
"Woman child, just remember your place!"
Even without a veil, they try to hide our face.

The children watch in budding fear.
They ask what we will be doing here.
We have seen history bent, but never broken.
We hold true to inspiring words, whenever spoken.

Compromise for us is not a four-letter word:
Working together for the good is never absurd.
We have come through storm and through fire.
Now is the time to stride higher and higher.

The people of Tennessee have a clear choice:
Let us work for victory with one united voice.
I won't let you take away my soul:
This is the essence of a woman's role.

This lesson we teach our children time after time:
Being born female must not be considered a crime.
Our brave ancestors planted the seeds.
Now we must fight to finish their deeds.

EVOLUTION - DEVOLUTION

'Nigger' just rolled off their tongues,
Full of hatred, denigration, and scorn.
They never understood the roots
From which the word had sprung.

'Token', like a drop of chocolate
Thrown into a bowl of buttermilk,
Stands out for its rarity, its strength,
Its sweetness that melts on the tongue.

'Affirmative Action' has such a positive tint,
Quietly reaffirms long-held prejudices, biases
That we be dumb, unworthy of honor or fame,
That all the hype of worthiness is to our blame.

'DEI' has become the latest in a litany of scorn,
Generational, institutional, bred in the blood.
No need to break the ancient mold, fired and hardened
In the kilns of history's rampage against the Other.

'Legacy' paints a line from past to present and
Encompasses all the vaunted glory of bygone generations.
All the inherited traits and points of view do not allow
For innovation or recalculations of the other's inherent worth.

'Networking' draws in all the spawn caught

Within a web of interconnected threads.
Networking binds friend of a friend into social strands tying
Like to like, eliminating alien growths from the inner circle of power.

'Meritocracy' proclaims and exclaims
That all straight White be right.
Anything else is all wrong in God's sight.
It leaves us free to hate and denigrate any who are not the same.

Race has never been in the blood, never in the face.
Race has always been only a marker
Of your starting place in the marathon of life.
It clearly shows others where you belong,

Embryonic hatred, never aborted, lives on
Only as a miscarriage of justice,
As the spawn of centuries' traditional preference
For pale reflections of humanity's mold.

23 July 2024

ABOUT THE AUTHOR

Ruby Jean Jones, Ph.D., is a dedicated educator, scholar, veteran, and linguist whose remarkable life journey reflects a deep commitment to learning, service, and cross-cultural understanding. Born on August 27, 1947, in Clarksdale, Mississippi, Dr. Jones began her academic journey with a Bachelor of Arts in Sociology from Coe College in 1969. Her career spans decades of service—from overseeing teenage girls at the Convent of the Good Shepherd to serving twenty years in the U.S. Army, where she specialized in military intelligence and Russian language instruction.

After retiring from the military in 1996, Dr. Jones pursued advanced studies in Slavic languages and literature, earning both her M.A. and Ph.D. from the University of Texas at Austin. Her dissertation, Echoing Their Lives: Teaching Russian Language and Culture Through the Music of Vladimir S. Vysotsky, reflects her unique passion for integrating music, culture, and language instruction.

As an accomplished linguist and independent scholar, she has taught at the Defense Language Institute in Monterey, California, and presented at conferences in the United States, Poland, and Sweden. Her academic work has been published in multiple languages, and her teaching has impacted students from diverse backgrounds—from young children to doctoral candidates.

This book is a heartfelt compilation of Dr. Jones's poetry, written over the course of her life. Through verse, she reflects on love, loss, identity, and the many facets of the human experience—offering readers a deeply personal glimpse into her journey across generations, cultures, and personal growth.

Since returning to Memphis in 2012, Dr. Jones has continued her service as a volunteer literacy tutor and reading mentor, while remaining active in her church and community. With decades of experience in teaching, translation, cultural scholarship, and service, Ruby Jean Jones exemplifies a life devoted to education, empowerment, and the enduring power of words.